D0459647

anythink

How Can I Deal With...?

Racism

Sally Hewitt

A⁺

Smart Apple Media

Smart Apple Media is published by
Black Rabbit Books
P.O. Box 3263, Mankato, Minnesota 56002

Printed in the United States

Published by arrangement with the Watts Publishing Group Ltd, London.

Library of Congress Cataloging-in-Publication Data

Hewitt, Sally, 1949–
    Racism / Sally Hewitt.
    p. cm.—(Smart Apple Media. How can I deal with—)
    Summary: "Case studies and helpful advice for kids who are bullied because of their race"—Provided by publisher.
    Includes bibliographical references and index.
    ISBN 978-1-59920-228-0
    1. Racism—United States—Juvenile literature. 2. Children of minorities—United States—Life skills guides—Juvenile literature. I. Title.
E184.A1W484 2009
305.800973—dc22
                    2007035715

Picture credits: Yolanda Chiaramello/Photofusion: 5. Bob Daemmrich/Imageworks/Topfoto: 22. Tony Freeman/Art Directors: 23. Spencer Grant/Art Directors: 29. Jeff Greenberg/Art Directors: 21. John Howard/Bubbles Photo Library: 16. Peter Hvizdak/Imageworks/Topfoto: 27. Mark Ludak/Imageworks/Topfoto: 8. Gideon Mendel/Corbis: front cover main. Brian Mitchell/Photofusion: 19, 20. David Montford/Photofusion: 14. Maggie Murray/Photofusion: 4. John Powell/Topfoto: 13. Ulrike Preuss/Photofusion: 7, 9. Ellen Senisi/Image Works/Topfoto: 10, 11, 12, 18. Israel Talby/Israel Images: 17. Topfoto: 6.

Series editor: Sarah Peutrill
Art director: Jonathan Hair
Design: Susi Martin
Picture research: Diana Morris
Series advisor: Sharon Lunney

Contents

I'm New in this Country and at School

Kwame is a new boy at school. He has just arrived from Ghana. He's learning English and he's shy because he can't speak English very well yet.

Marek's Story

Kwame is in my class. I'm from Poland and I know what it feels like to be new and learning a new language. I want to be Kwame's friend, but I don't know if he wants to be mine.

Kwame's Story

I'm learning English but the other children talk so quickly! They laugh when I make a face if I don't understand them. I was smart at my school in Ghana and got good grades. But I don't feel smart here.

I want to play soccer.

I was captain of my class team in Ghana.

When the kids were choosing a team at recess, one of them pointed at me and said, "Don't choose him, he's stupid." I understood him when he said that!

What Can Kwame Do?

The children are being unfair to Kwame by not giving him a chance. He can:

- ✔ talk to his mom and dad,
- ✔ tell them not being good at English makes him feel shy and not smart,
- ✔ say he finds it difficult to make friends, and
- ✔ say he wants to play soccer!

What Kwame Did

I talked to Dad. He talked to my teacher. She helped me tell the children about my school in Ghana. I showed them photos of me playing soccer! Now I'm always chosen to play soccer and everyone knows I'm not stupid. My English is getting better every day, and Marek is my best friend.

Miss Everard's Story

When Kwame first came to school, he only spoke a little English. The other children didn't help him or spend time getting to know him. But he was so good and worked so hard, I didn't realize he was unhappy. I'm glad his mom and dad talked to me.

Kwame told the children about his school in Ghana, and they asked him lots of questions. Now that they know more about him, they have been kinder and more helpful.

We Are Different and the Same

All over the world, people speak different languages and look different from each other. They have different religions and cultures, but everyone belongs to the human race.

Imagine how boring the world would be if we were all exactly the same.

By respecting and learning from each other, we can live and work together happily and peacefully.

I'm Left Out

Faiza is a Muslim. Most of her school friends are not Muslims. When they don't invite her to do things with them after school, she feels left out.

Ellie's Story

Faiza is my new friend at school. We sat together at sports day yesterday. But my other friends say she's not allowed to have fun like us. Sometimes she wears different clothes than us. They say if we invited her to parties and sleepovers, she would spoil everything.

Faiza's Story

My school friends do things together after school, but they never ask me to join in.

When they talk about the fun they had, I feel left out. They say, "Oh you wouldn't enjoy it Faiza. You're a Muslim."

They think because I'm a Muslim, I'm not allowed to watch television or play computer games or listen to music. They think my mom and dad are very strict so they don't want to come to my house.

What Can Faiza Do?

It would help if Faiza's friends understood her religion better.

She can:
- ✔ tell her mom and dad what her friends think,
- ✔ tell her friends why she sometimes wears different clothes than they do, and
- ✔ say she wants to join in with them more.

What Faiza Did

My mom talked to my teacher and to Ellie's mom. My teacher invited my mom to talk about our religion at school. Mom was shy, but she was brilliant and everyone liked her. They understand us much better now. Ellie's been over to my house and I've been over to hers. We had lots of fun!

What Is Racism?

Racism is treating people differently, unfairly, or unkindly just because they are different. There are all kinds of ways of being

different. People have different colored skin, speak different languages, or have different religions and cultures.

Racism can be saying unkind things, leaving someone out, ruining their things, or hurting them.

Both children and adults may be racist. But racism is a kind of bullying. It is never all right to be racist.

It's My Home Too!

Dipti's dad comes from India, but she was born in this country. She was shocked when someone told her to go back to where she came from.

Gemma's Story

I was playing with Dipti when some kids in our class said, "Go back where you came from, Dipti!"

I asked Dipti, "Where do you come from?"

She said, "Here! The same as you." Then she cried. I didn't mean to upset her.

Dipti's Story

My brother and I were born in this country, the same as Gemma. Then she asked where I came from because of what some kids at school said! I was really upset and cross with her. Just because I have different colored skin, they think this isn't my home. But it is!

Connor's family came from Ireland, but he was born here too. No one says, "Go back where you came from!" to Connor. I think that's because he has the same colored skin as them.

What Can Dipti Do?

The children said a racist thing to Dipti. They didn't bother to find out about her— they thought they already knew.

She can:

✔ tell Gemma why she's upset by her question, and

✔ tell her teacher what the children said.

What Dipti Did

I told Gemma why she upset me and she was really sorry. We're best friends again now. Gemma came with me to talk to our teacher.

Our teacher asked us all to make a family tree. We found that lots of us had parents and grandparents from all over the world, not just me!

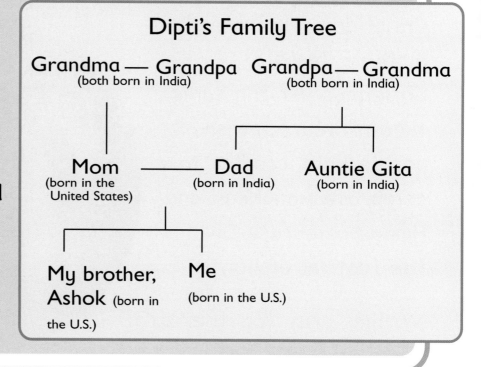

Dipti's Family Tree

Grandma — Grandpa (both born in India)   Grandpa — Grandma (both born in India)

Mom (born in the United States) — Dad (born in India)   Auntie Gita (born in India)

My brother, Ashok (born in the U.S.)   Me (born in the U.S.)

Celebrations

A Principal's Story

Children in our school come from many different backgrounds. We learn about our different religions and respect each other's special celebrations.

Christians celebrate the birth of Jesus at Christmas. At the same time of year, Jewish people light candles to celebrate Hanukkah and Hindus celebrate Divali, the festival of lights.

Muslims pray together at Friday prayers. Friday sunset to Saturday sunset is the Jewish holy day. Christians go to church on Sunday. It's nice to know we've got so many things to celebrate!

Brad's Story

For my birthday, I planned a bowling party and a sleepover. All my friends said they would come—except David. He said, "I can't, it's the Sabbath."

We gave David a hard time about that!

I told my dad that David couldn't come—just because it's Sabbath! But Dad explained that David is Jewish and that Sabbath is important in his religion. They have a family meal together on Friday nights. I felt bad about giving David a hard time.

Dad said, "We can go another night so David can come too." So we did and David came. I said sorry to David and we're friends again now.

Racism Is Making My Friend Unhappy

Reggie's friend Shen is being teased about his name. Reggie doesn't want his friend to be unhappy. He wants to do something to help him.

Reggie's Story

My friend Shen's mom and dad are from China. He was born in the same hospital on the same day as me! We have joint birthday parties. We've always been friends and so have our moms.

"It's my name!"

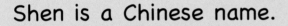

Shen is a Chinese name.

Some children in our school started calling Shen lots of different names they thought sounded Chinese like Ching and Wong. They thought it was funny.

But he didn't laugh. He got angry.

I said to him, "It's only a name!"

But Shen said, "It's my name! I'm not just a Chinese boy. I'm me and my name is Shen!"

I can see what he means. My grandad's name is Reginald. I'm named after him and I'm proud of my name.

What Can Reggie Do?

Making fun of Shen's Chinese name is a kind of racism. Reggie can help stop it.

He can:
- ✔ try to imagine how Shen feels,
- ✔ tell Shen he understands and that he'll stand up for him, and
- ✔ help stop the other children calling Shen the wrong names.

What Reggie Did

When the children started calling Shen the wrong name, I told them it was unkind and they should stop. They just laughed and went on doing it. Shen and I pretended not to hear.

Shen never, ever answered to the wrong name. They soon got bored and stopped. Shen is much happier now.

I'm in a Gang

Binh is in a gang. All his friends live in the same part of town and share the same culture. They are unfriendly to children who aren't the same as them.

Marvin's Story

Binh used to be my friend. He isn't friendly to me any more because he's in a gang that I'm not allowed to join. His gang friends think they're better than everyone else!

Binh's Story

I was proud to be in the gang. We all live near each other and our parents all come from Vietnam.

When Marvin wanted to do things with us, the gang wouldn't let him.

They said, "You're not one of us!" Then they said stuff about the color of his skin and other unkind things.

Marvin didn't like that. I didn't like it either, but I didn't say anything. I can't be in the gang and be Marvin's friend, too.

What Can Binh Do?

Not letting someone join your gang because of where they come from or the color of their skin is racism.
He can:

✔ think about how Marvin feels,

✔ remember Marvin was his friend first, and

✔ ask himself if he wants to be in a gang that won't include his friend.

What Binh Did

I decided I didn't want to be in a gang if my best friend couldn't be in it, too.

Marvin agreed with me and we just walked away. I felt good about that—and so did Marvin. We've made lots more friends, too. Now that we've stood up to the gang, maybe they'll stop behaving like racist bullies.

I'm Scared

A gang is frightening Bilal and his little sister Nasreen. Nasreen wants to tell their mom and dad, but Bilal says she can't tell anyone.

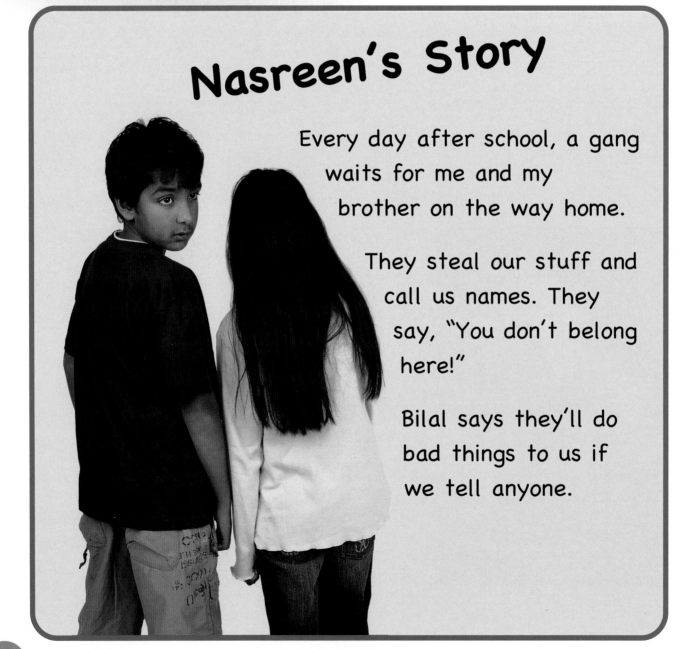

Nasreen's Story

Every day after school, a gang waits for me and my brother on the way home.

They steal our stuff and call us names. They say, "You don't belong here!"

Bilal says they'll do bad things to us if we tell anyone.

Bilal's Story

I feel really afraid of a gang of racist bullies. They push me and Nasreen and say bad things to us. If we have any money or anything they like the look of, they just steal it! I want to tell someone, but they say they'll hurt Nasreen if I do.

So I made Nasreen promise not to tell. Now I think she's a bit scared of me as well. But it's my job to look after my little sister! I don't know what to do.

What Can Bilal and Nasreen Do?

They can't beat the bullies on their own, but no one can help them if they don't say anything. They can:

✔ make a diary of what the gang does every day, and

✔ tell their parents or a grown-up they trust and show them the diary.

What Bilal Did

I told our parents. They said, "We can't deal with this on our own."

They told the school and the police, and the gang was punished.

An adult walks home with us every day. We feel safe now, and the gang didn't win.

Racism in Schools

All schools have rules about racism. Felicity had a special lesson about it.

Felicity's Story

At school, our class discussed how racism hurts people. We agreed racism is always wrong and that we wouldn't do or say racist things.

If we see anyone being racist, even an adult, we can tell someone about it. Sometimes we can stop racism happening to us by standing up to the bullies. Or we can keep calm and walk away. But we often need help from a grown-up.

Our school has strict rules about racism. Teachers or other members of staff will always help if we go to them.

We Dealt with Racism

Mel made racist comments about Aleesha when she first came to school. She tried to stop Aleesha from making new friends.

Mel and Aleesha's Story

Aleesha: I missed my friends at my old school, but I thought I'd soon make new friends at my new school. I was getting along well, but then Mel started saying racist things about me!

Mel: When Aleesha first came to school, my friends thought she was really cool. They all wanted to be her friend. I was jealous so I said racist things to try and turn them against her. The racist comments worked! Some of my friends even joined in being unkind to Aleesha.

Aleesha: When I heard what Mel and her friends were saying about me, I was upset and angry. I wanted to shout at Mel but I thought, "That won't make the other children like me."

Mel: My plan was going well, until Sam said I shouldn't say racist things about Aleesha.

Aleesha: I didn't have to shout at Mel because Sam stood up for me. It was great!

Mel: I was angry and upset with Sam, and I told him so. He said, "Now you know how Aleesha feels!" I hadn't thought about how Aleesha was feeling.

Aleesha: Mel's friends started being nice to me and being unkind to her! So now I felt sorry for her.

Mel: I decided to say sorry to Aleesha. I don't like saying sorry, and it was difficult. But she was really cool about it.

Aleesha: Mel and I both know how it feels when someone makes racist comments. It isn't nice. I've made lots of new friends now, and Mel is one of them!

Glossary

Celebration
A festival, party, meal, or religious service held on a day that is special to a group of people or a religion.

Culture
The culture of a country is its art, music, ideas, and beliefs.

Family tree
A family tree is a diagram shaped like a tree that shows how the members of a family are related to each other and when they were born.

Gang
A gang is a group of friends who hang out together and have similar interests.

Jewish
Someone who is Jewish follows the religion of Judaism.

Language
The language of a country is how the people speak. For example, the English language is spoken in England and the United States. The Chinese language is spoken in China.

Muslim
A Muslim is a believer in the religion of Islam.

Race
A race is a group of people who come from the same part of the world.

Racism
Racism is when a person or group of people are treated badly because of their race.

Religion
A religion is a set of beliefs about god. Christianity, Islam, Hinduism, Sikhism, Judaism, and Buddhism are all religions.

Sabbath
The Sabbath is a holy day of rest and worship in Judaism.

Further Information

For Kids:
http://www.kidshealth.org/kid/feeling/emotion/bullies.html
Learn about bullies and how to deal with them.

http://www.tolerance.org/pt/index.html
Find cool games and stories on this site that help you learn to understand different cultures.

http://www.kidlink.org/english/voice/racism/index.html
Read comments from kids around the world about why we should stop racism.

For Parents:
http://www.ymca.net/resources_for_families/children_and_ cultural_diversity.html
Tips for parents to help their kids be tolerant toward other cultures.

http://mentalhealth.samhsa.gov/15plus/parent/
The National Mental Health Information Center offers articles for parents to help kids deal with bullies.

For Teachers:
http://www.teachablemoment.org/toolbox/toughtimestoolbox.html
This site offers tips for addressing tough issues in your classroom and for helping kids express their feelings.

http://www.pbs.org/kcts/preciouschildren/diversity/index.html
This site has resources for teachers, including activities that promote racial awareness and how to deal with insensitivity.

Note to parents and teachers: Every effort has been made by the publishers to ensure that these Web sites are suitable for children, that they are of the highest educational value, and that they contain no inappropriate or offensive material. However, because of the nature of the Internet, it is impossible to guarantee that the contents of these sites will not be altered. We strongly advise that Internet access is supervised by a responsible adult.

Index

Notes for Parents, Caregivers, and Teachers

Children can experience racist bullying simply because they are different in some way. It might be because they belong to a different race or culture or because of their religion or even their accent. There are many ways parents, caregivers, and teachers can help children deal with racism.
- Children need to know racism is always wrong.
- If a child is experiencing racism, it is not his fault.
- Building up a child's self-esteem is helpful.
- Fear of making things worse can stop children telling anyone. They need to know that the adult they tell will take effective action.

Page 5 Kwame's Story
The children in Kwame's class have decided he is stupid because he's still learning to speak English.
- Children can be encouraged to get to know each other properly and not to make judgements about other children because they are different.

Page 9 Faiza's Story
Faiza feels left out because her friends don't understand her religion even though they think they do.
- Understanding each other's religion and culture can help children to have fun together and respect any differences at the same time.

Page 13 Dipti's Story
Dipti is upset because she has been told to "Go back where she came from!"
- Children should understand that this is a racist comment. It is hurtful and never acceptable.

Page 17 Brad's Story
Brad was unkind to his friend because of his religion.
- It's kinder and more helpful to find a way around a difference than to create a conflict over it.

Page 18 Reggie's Story
Reggie's friend is unhappy because he is being called the wrong name.
- Laughing at someone's name because it sounds foreign is upsetting. Calling someone by their proper name shows you respect them.

Page 21 Binh's Story
Binh's gang is excluding Marvin because he isn't one of them.
- Gangs based on race can lead to racist behavior against other people. Children should be encouraged to include any child in their group of friends.

Page 25 Nasreen and Bilal's Story
Nasreen and Bilal are being intimidated by a gang.
- This kind of racism needs effective intervention from an adult. Fear of walking to and from school can be a sign that children are being bullied.

Page 28 Mel and Aleesha's Story
Children could role-play the parts in this simple script. They could also write and perform their own play about racism.